# The Irresistible Rose is Rose

## A Collection of *Rose is Rose* Comics

### by Pat Brady

**Andrews McMeel
Publishing**

Kansas City

00 01 02 03 04  BAH  10 9 8 7 6 5 4 3 2 1

ISBN:  0-7407-0554-7

Library of Congress Catalog Card Number:  00-103473

Read *Rose is Rose* Online: www.comics.com

E-Mail Pat Brady: PBradyRose@aol.com

────── **ATTENTION:  SCHOOLS AND BUSINESSES** ──────

Andrews McMeel books are available at quantity discounts with bulk purchase for educational, business, or sales promotional use.  For information, please write to: Special Sales Department, Andrews McMeel Publishing, 4520 Main Street, Kansas City, Missouri  64111.

**Other *Rose is Rose* Books by Pat Brady**

She's a Momma, Not a Movie Star

License to Dream

Rose is Rose 15th Anniversary Collection

**FLIP THE PAGES WITH YOUR LEFT THUMB AND WATCH ROSE RETURN TO CHILDHOOD!**

FLIP THE PAGES WITH YOUR RIGHT THUMB AND WATCH ROSE'S ALTER EGO EMERGE!

ONE
PERSON'S
VIEW
DURING
SYNCHRONIZED
CARTWHEELS

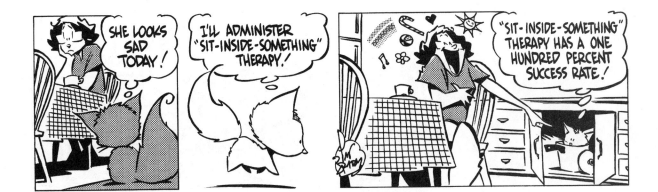

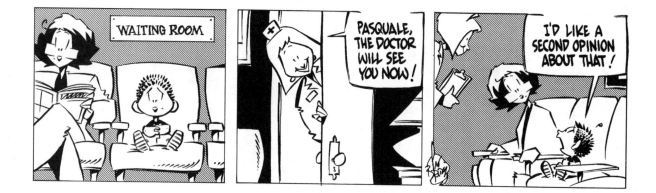

"LIGHTING SPECIALIST"
AMAZING MOMMA SKILL #4267-C

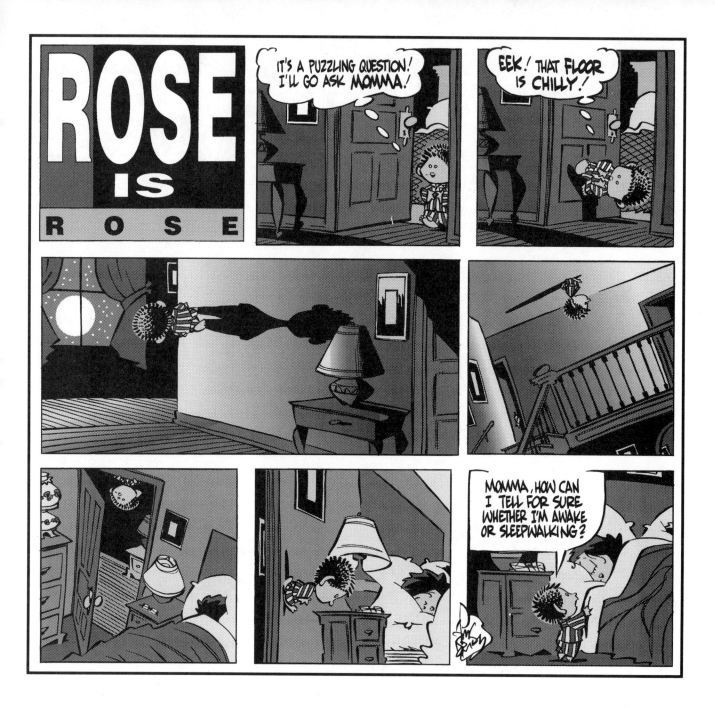

20

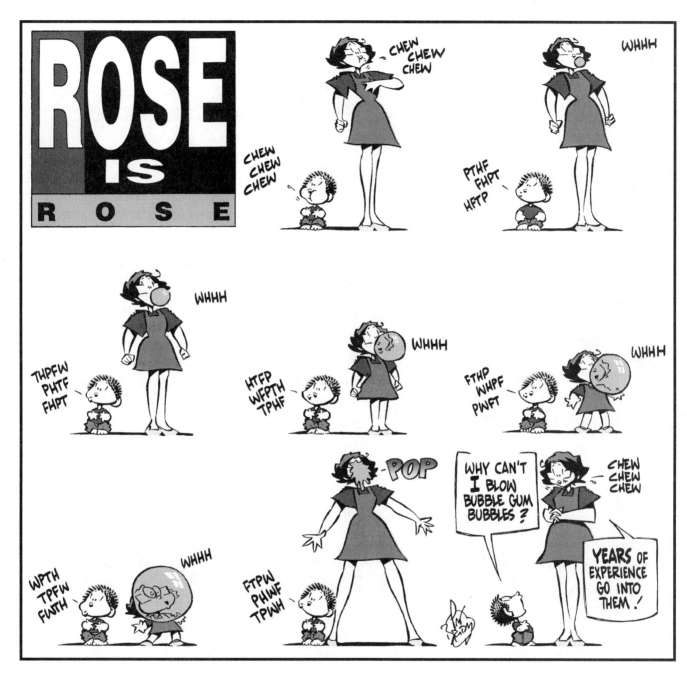

FLIP THE PAGES WITH YOUR LEFT THUMB AND WATCH ROSE RETURN TO CHILDHOOD!

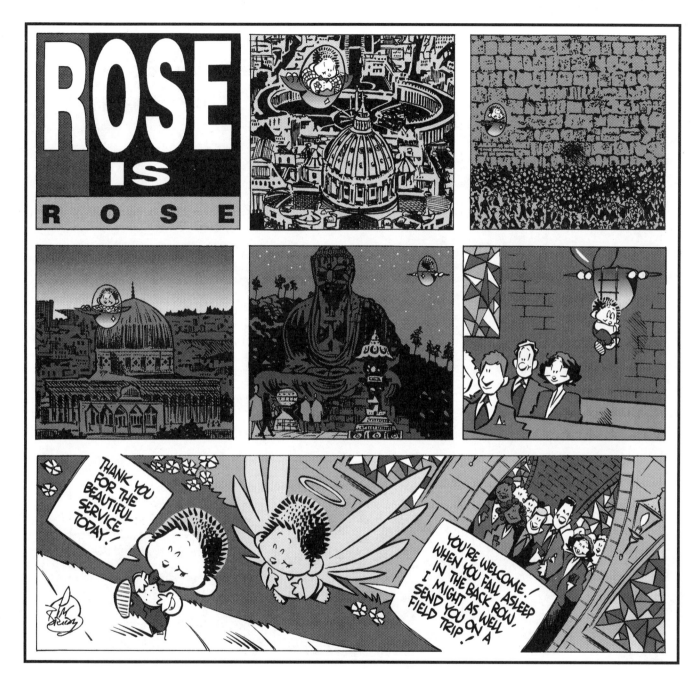

FLIP THE PAGES WITH YOUR RIGHT THUMB AND WATCH ROSE'S ALTER EGO EMERGE!

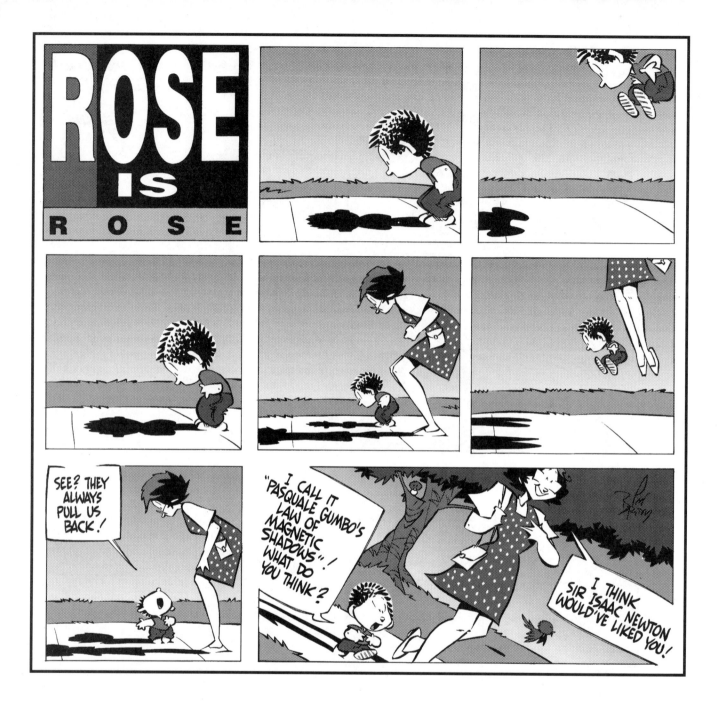

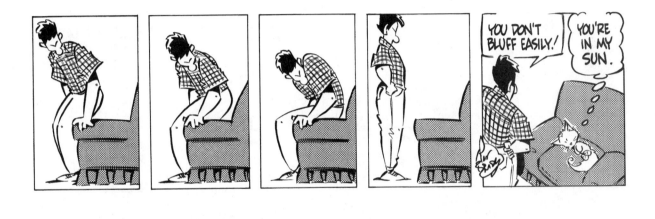

FLIP THE PAGES WITH YOUR LEFT THUMB AND WATCH ROSE RETURN TO CHILDHOOD!

FLIP THE PAGES WITH YOUR RIGHT THUMB AND WATCH ROSE'S ALTER EGO EMERGE!

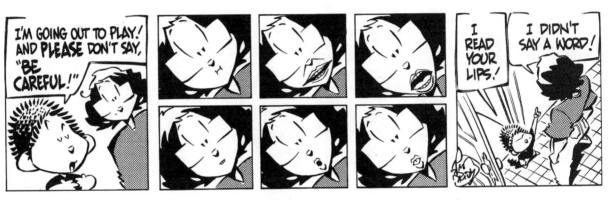

TAIL PERFORMANCE ART

CLAP
CLAP
CLAP
CLAP
CLAP

CRASH

TAIL PERFORMANCE ART CAN BE RUINED BY A DISTRACTING NOISE BACKSTAGE.

WHAT ARE THOSE THINGS?

OH... THEY'RE "MISTER POTATO HEAD" NOSES!

MIMI SOMETIMES USES DECOYS WHEN HUNTING FOR NOSES TO GRAB.

WISDOM FROM MAHARISHI PEEKABOO:

:PURR:

WATCHING RESTLESS THOUGHTS COME AND GO IS THE ESSENCE OF MEDITATION.

:PURR:

WISDOM FROM MAHARISHI PEEKABOO: AFTER LONG PERIODS OF MEDITATING...

PURR PURR PURR

SPONTANEOUS LEVITATION MAY OCCUR...

PURR PURR PURR

PURR PURR

WHILE THE PHENOMENON MAY BE MOMENTARILY EXHILARATING...

IT OFTEN LEADS TO THE LOSS OF A GOOD MEDITATION SPOT.

:MUNCH:
:GULP: :CLINK: :SIP:
:CLINK: :CHEW:

I'D LIKE ANOTHER HELPING OF **TIME**, PLEASE!

ME TOO!

ME TOO!

IT'S A DELIGHTFUL RECIPE... AND SO **LIGHT**!

I UNDERSTAND OVERINDULGENCE IS HEALTHFUL!

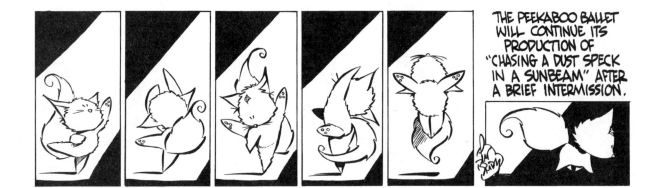

PORTRAIT
OF
ONE CAT
AND
TWO
CIRCLING
MOSQUITOS

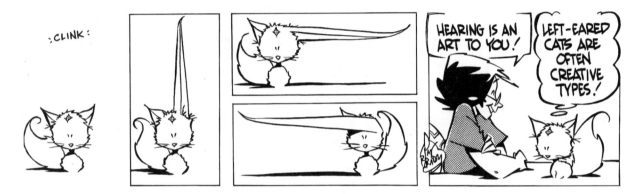

FLIP THE PAGES WITH YOUR LEFT THUMB AND WATCH ROSE RETURN TO CHILDHOOD!

**FLIP THE PAGES WITH YOUR RIGHT THUMB AND WATCH ROSE'S ALTER EGO EMERGE!**

ONLY THE MOST ELITE, WORLD CLASS CATS EVER ATTEMPT THE DANGEROUS "TRIPLE OOPS"!

THE SLOW MOTION REPLAY OF PEEKABOO'S "TRIPLE OOPS" REVEALS A MOMENTARY LOSS OF COMPOSURE

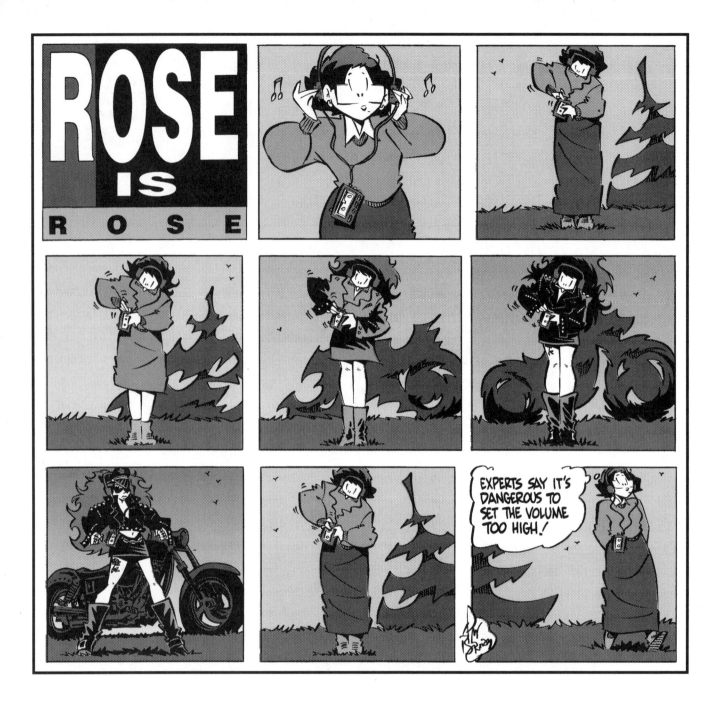

FLIP THE PAGES WITH YOUR LEFT THUMB AND WATCH ROSE RETURN TO CHILDHOOD!

86

**FLIP THE PAGES WITH YOUR RIGHT THUMB AND WATCH ROSE'S ALTER EGO EMERGE!**

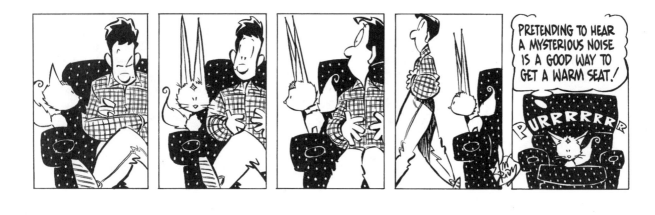

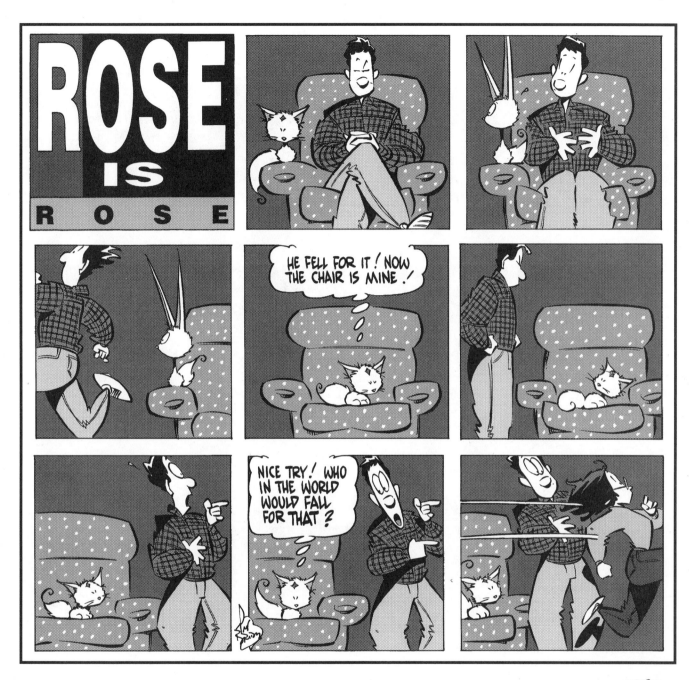

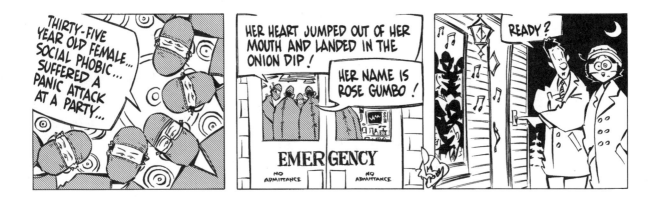

94

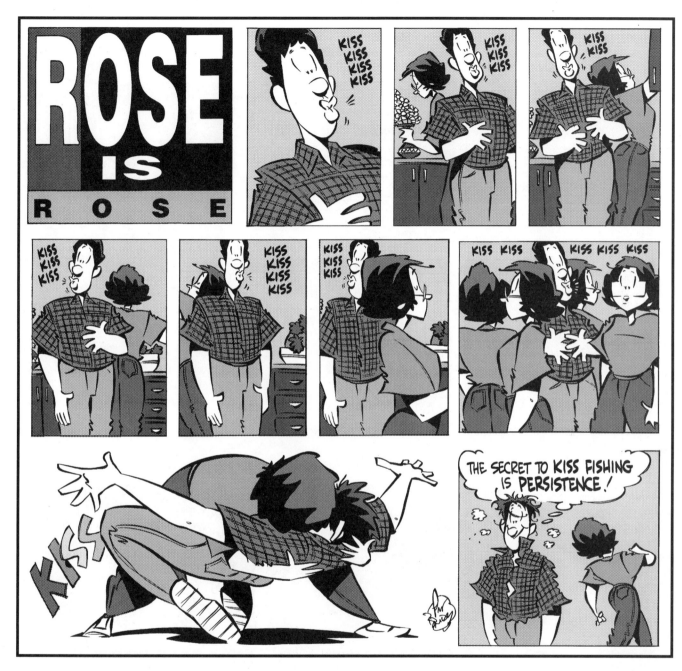

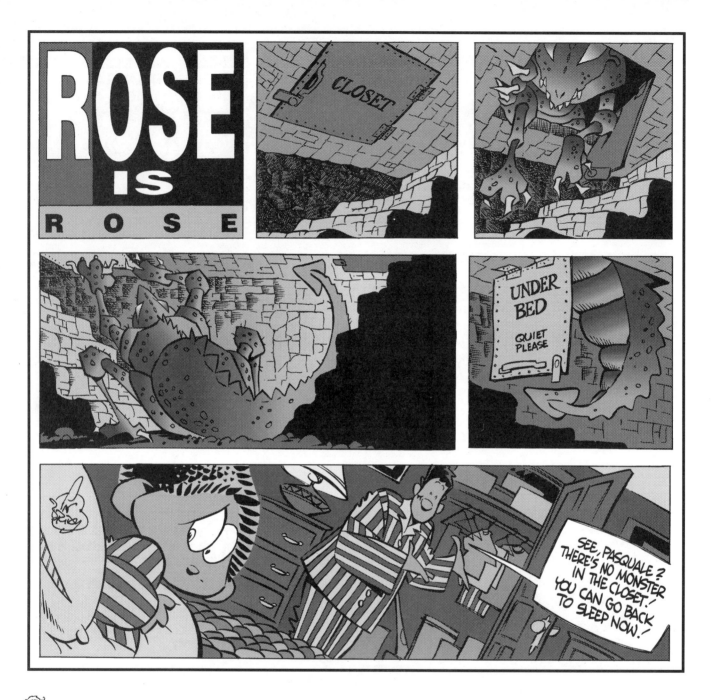

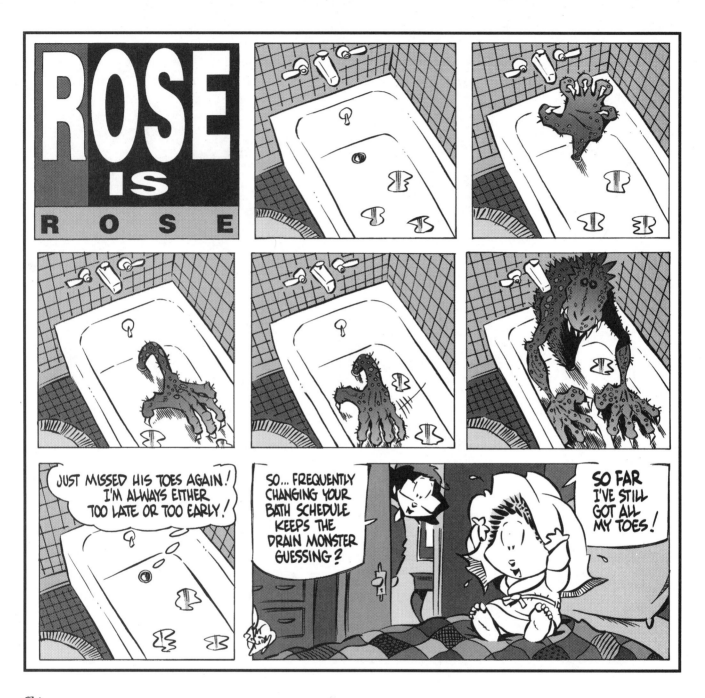

TEA STEAM, SNOW AND KITTEN FOOTSTEPS: THREE FINALISTS IN THE **QUIETNESS** COMPETITION

EXCUSE ME, I HAVE ANOTHER SQUEEZE COMING IN!

"SQUEEZE WAITING" IS AVAILABLE TO ALL SQUEEZE CUSTOMERS!

YOU CAN'T AFFORD TO MISS AN IMPORTANT SQUEEZE!

SOME LOVE THE OUTDOORS

SOME LOVE THE INDOORS

AH, BUT GIVE ME THE GREAT BETWEENDOORS!

MAKE UP YOUR MIND!

**FLIP THE PAGES WITH YOUR LEFT THUMB AND WATCH ROSE RETURN TO CHILDHOOD!**

**FLIP THE PAGES WITH YOUR RIGHT THUMB AND WATCH ROSE'S ALTER EGO EMERGE!**

119

FLIP THE PAGES WITH YOUR LEFT THUMB AND WATCH ROSE RETURN TO CHILDHOOD!

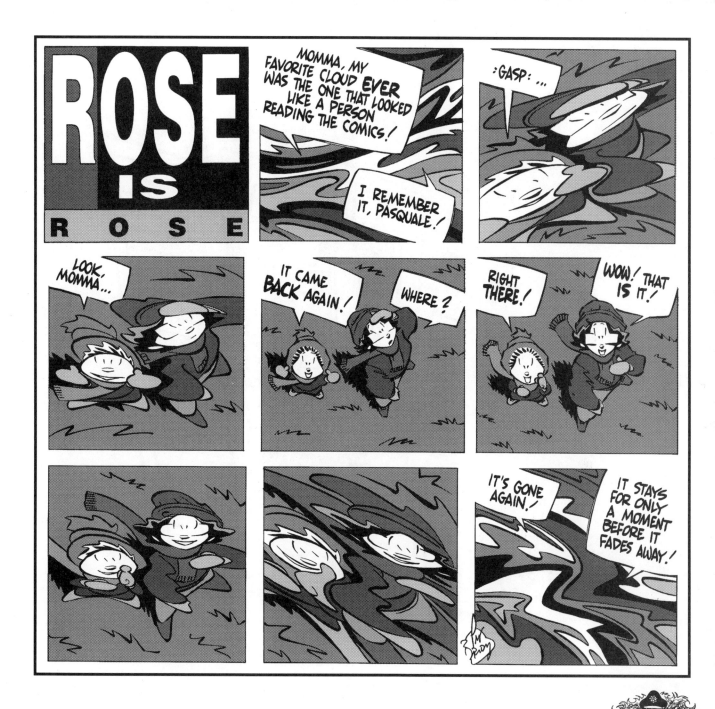

**FLIP THE PAGES WITH YOUR RIGHT THUMB AND WATCH ROSE'S ALTER EGO EMERGE!**